AF578946

52 Haiku

Reflections From Life In Colorado

Doris A McCraw

Chinook Mountain Publishing

Copyright © 2022 by Doris A. McCraw

All rights reserved.

No portion of this book may be reproduced in any form without written permission from the publisher or author, except as permitted by U.S. copyright law.

Contents

1

Natural Destruction

Nature's destruction
An end, or new beginning
The phoenix rises

2

Natural Destruction

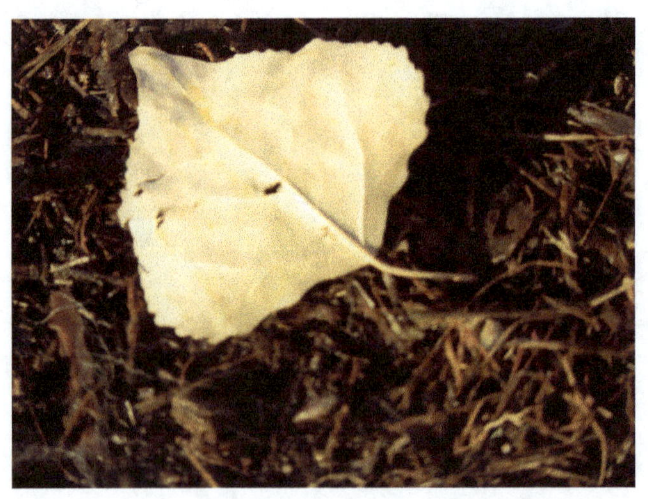

3

Life As A Lie

Live life as a lie
Like artificial flowers
A rose with no scent

4

Life As A Lie

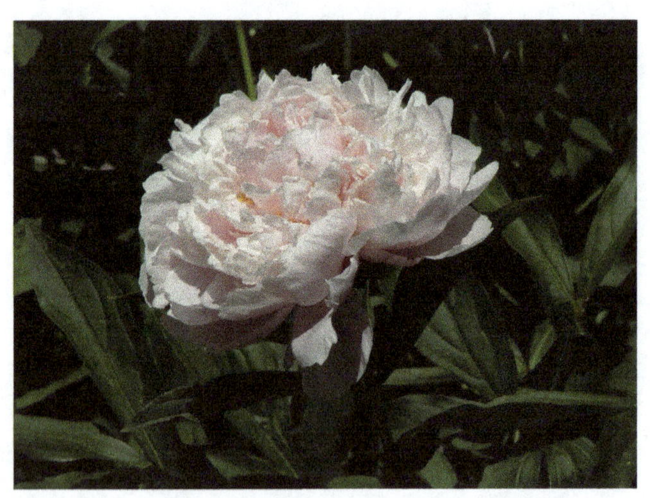

5

Wonderful Journey

Wonderful journey
Despite heartache, pain, and loss
Watching for blessings.

6

Wonderful Journey

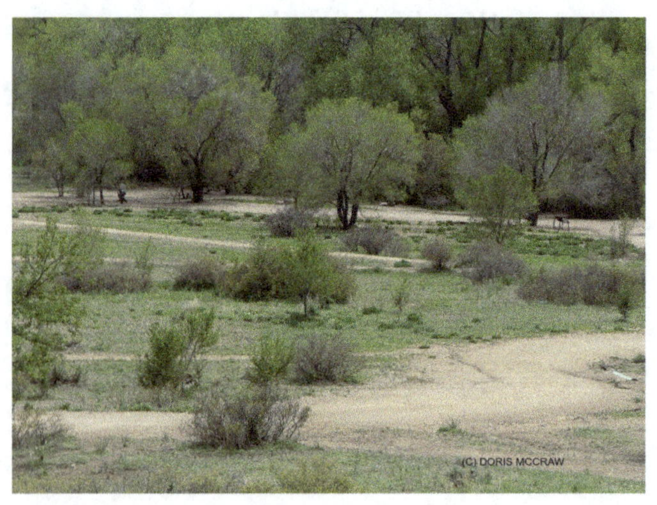

7

Letting Go

Learning to let go
Memories will always be
Each sunset is new

8

Letting Go

9

Small Disappointments

Small disappointments
Of seasons expectations
Relax, enjoy life

10

Small Disappointments

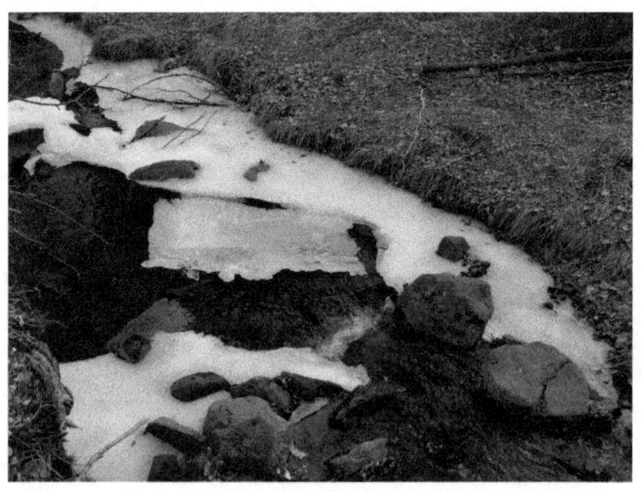

11

Laughing

Full moon lying low
Laughing at the world's antics
We can laugh also

12

Laughing

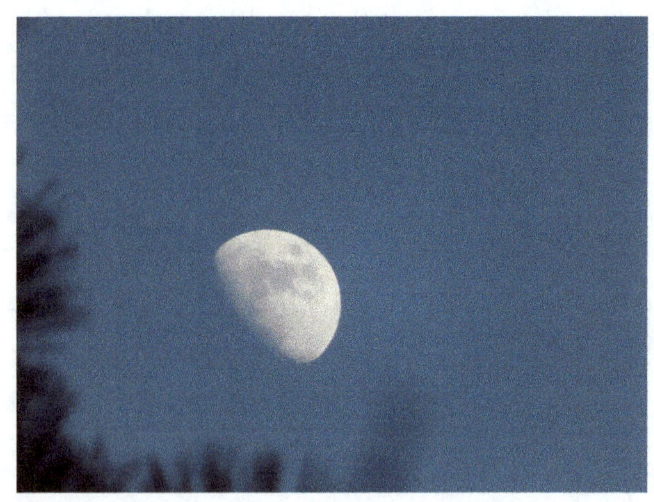

13

Agitation

Agitated world
Focused on all that is wrong
Small stone into large

14

Agitation

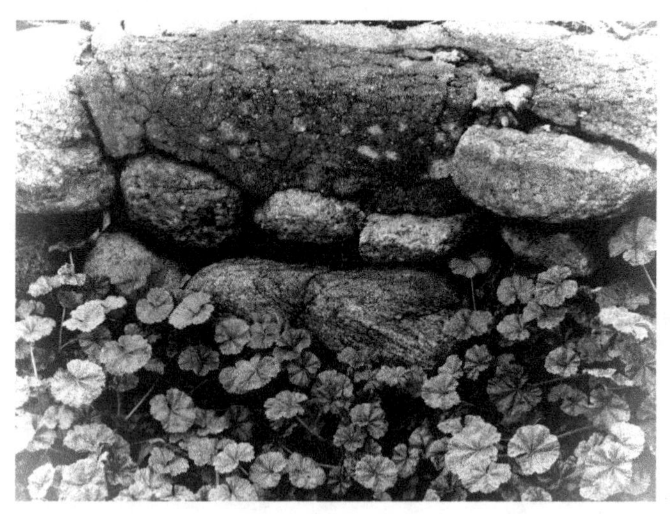

15

Igniting Dreams

Igniting the dream
Integrating heart and mind
Walking your own path

16

Igniting Dreams

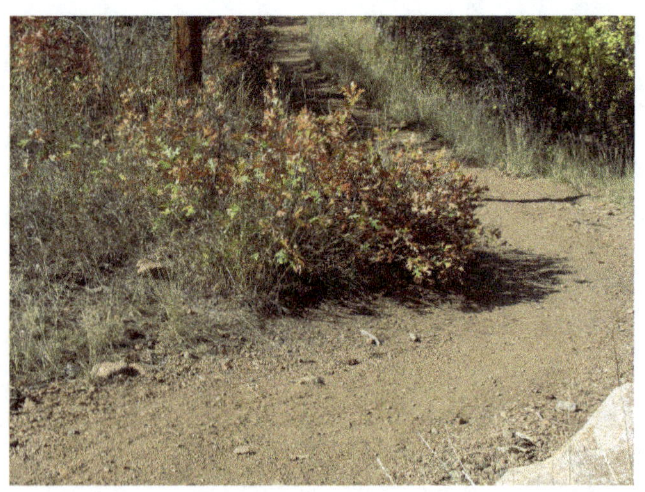

17

Naked History

Naked history
Telling stories from the facts
See different trees

18

Naked History

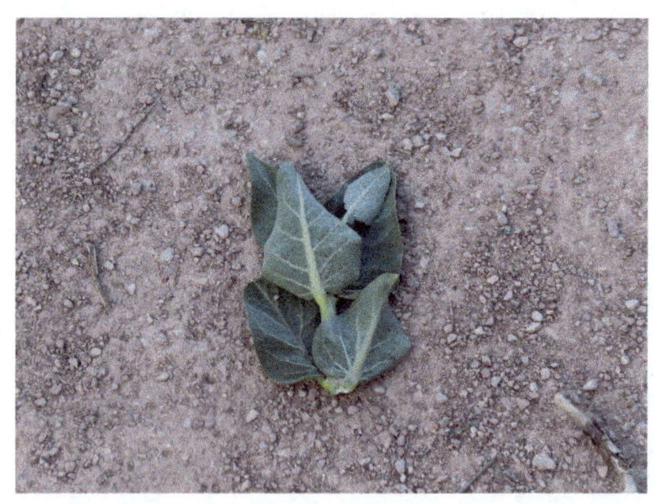

19

Dream

Becoming the dream
Ghost from the past lead the way
Pod remains, seeds gone

20

Dream

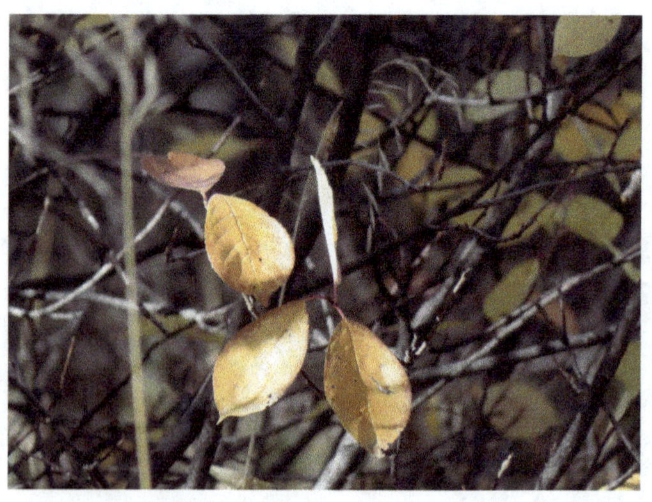

21

Siren Call

The wild siren calls
A responding deep within
Washed on waves of dreams

22

Siren Call

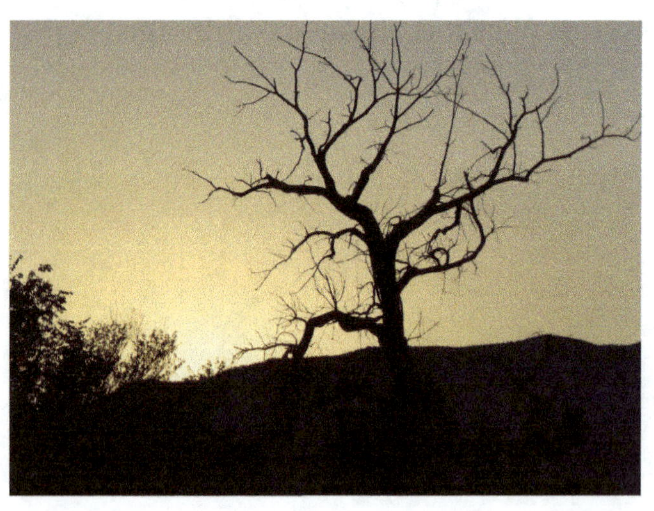

23

Life and Laughter

Life full of laughter
Quickest way to live a dream
Water and ice glow

24

Life and Laughter

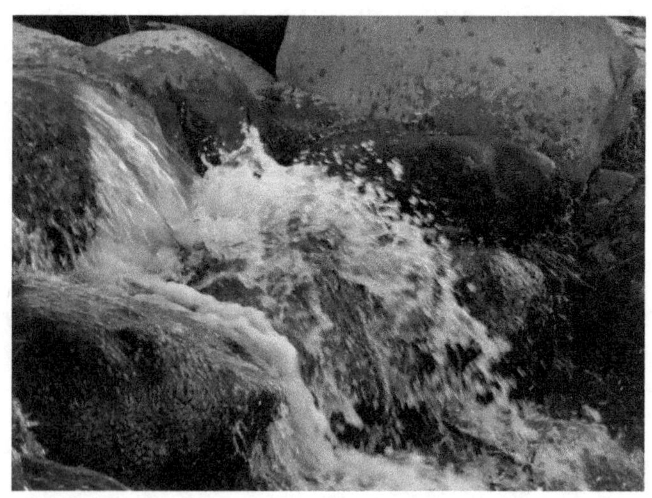

25

Seeds

Day of memory
Honoring what was before
Soon buds turn to seeds

26

Seeds

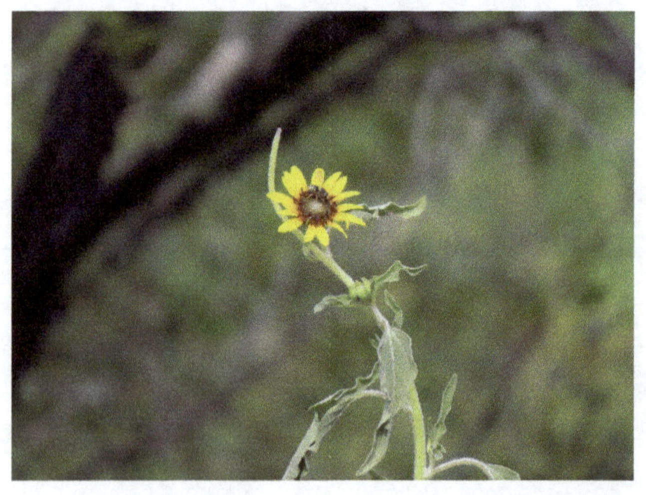

27

History Lesson

A history lesson
Traveling high lonesome roads
To reach far-flung peaks

28

History Lesson

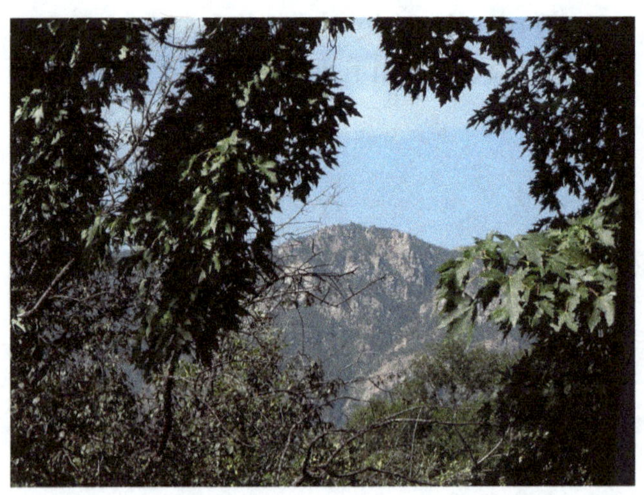

29

Life Amid Decay

Life amid decay
Flowing like water through hands
Sing an ode to joy

30

Life Amid Decay

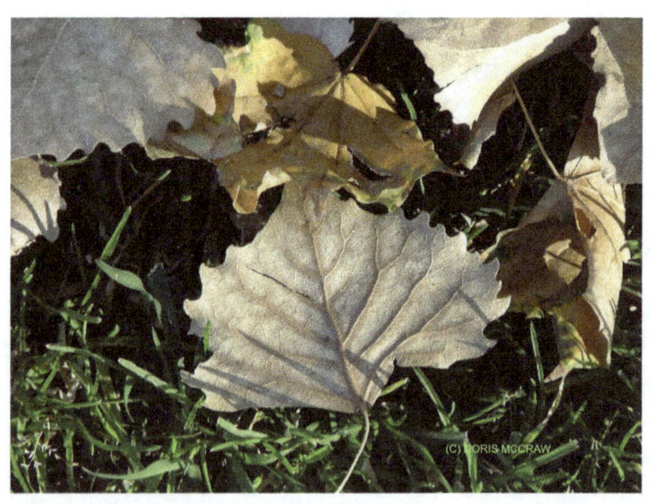

***

31

In Society

In society
We search for a destiny
A barren landscape

32

In Society

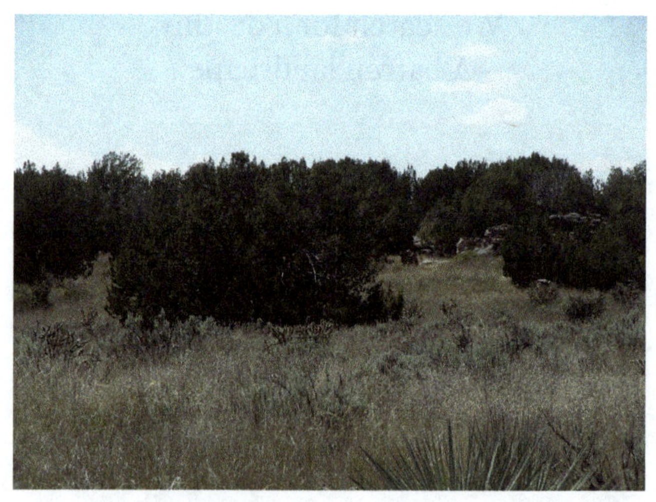

33

White Peaks

To a far white peak
During an uncommon time
Focused on the goal

34

White Peaks

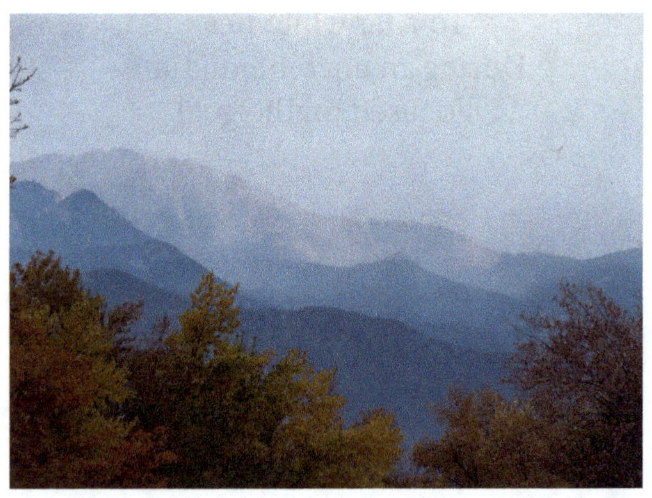

35

Discovery

A discovery
The joyful expedition
Foundation of life

36

Discovery

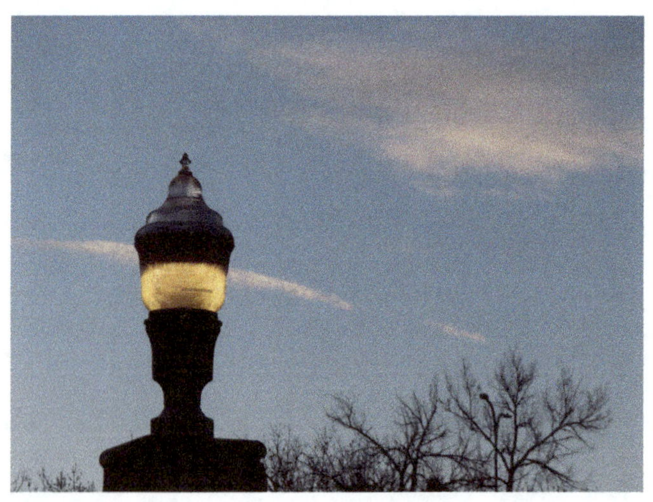

37

Deep Longing

Heart knows deep longing
High mountain valley landscape
Fills a willing mind

38

Deep Longing

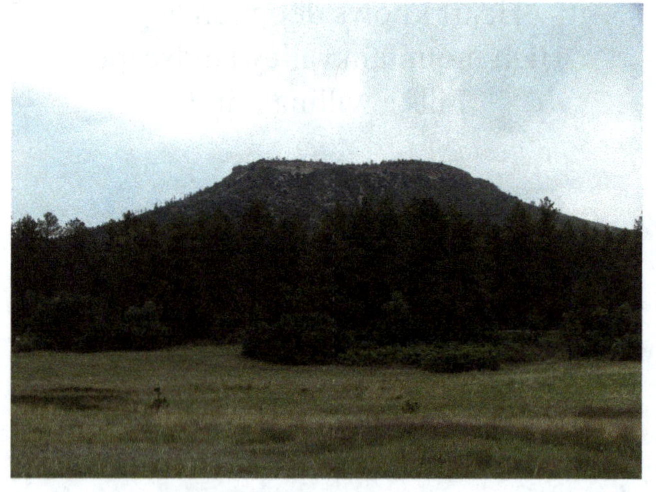

39

Anger

What brings on anger?
Uncaring, being ignored?
Fly above it all.

40

Anger

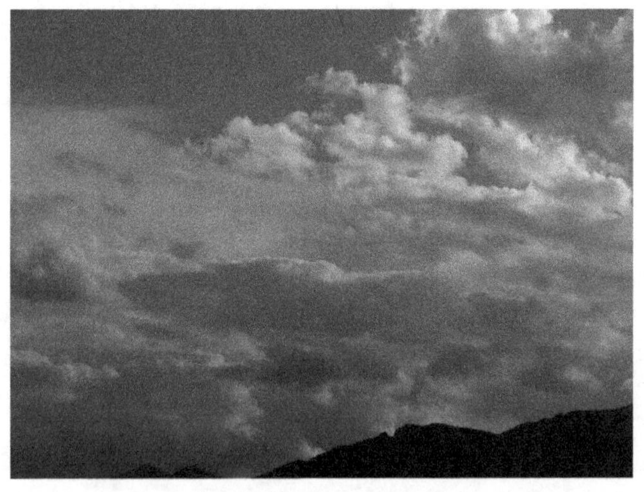

41

Lost in Shadows

Lost in the shadows
Searching through deep thoughts of fear
Clear skies behind clouds

42

Lost in Shadows

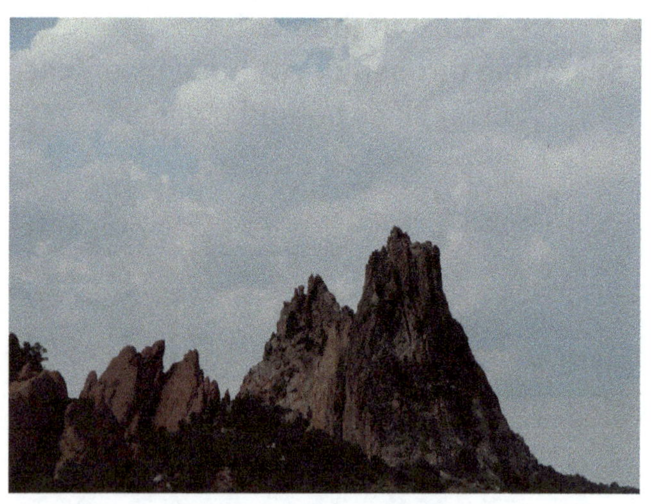

43

Perspective

All is perspective
Mountains becoming molehills
Why live high drama

44

Perspective

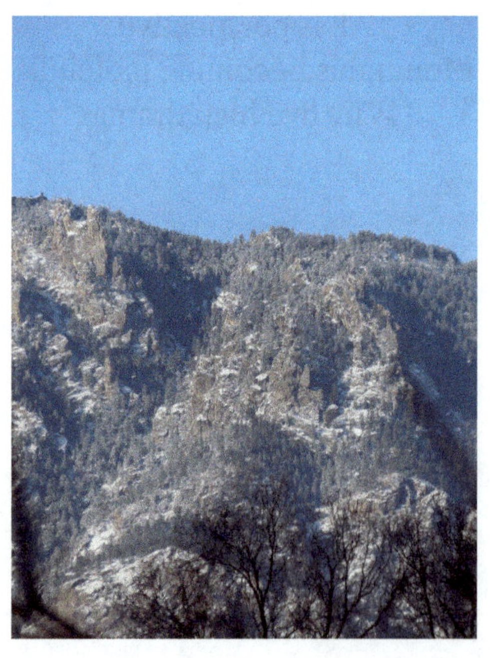

45

Watching

Life creates chaos
The mind strives to understand
Watch the gentle stream

46

Watching

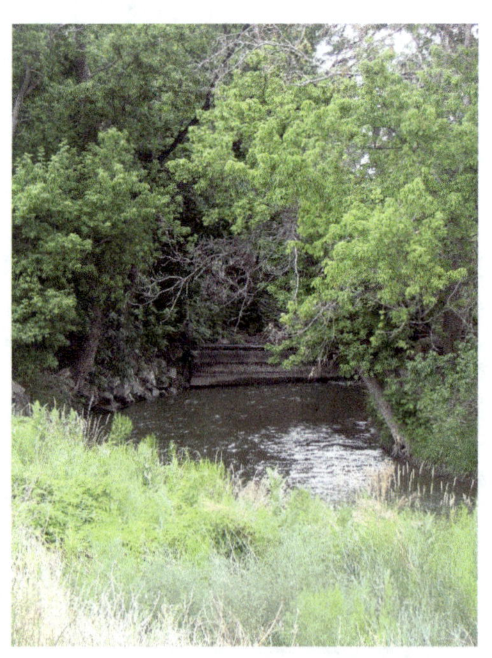

47

Cherish

Cherish memories
Look forward to the future
Truth is where you look

48

Cherish

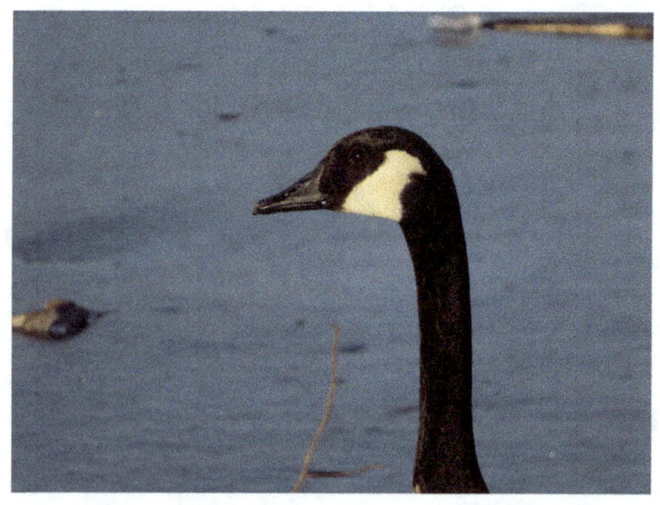

49

Grace

Each moment of life
Opportunity for grace
Sometimes it's hidden

50

Grace

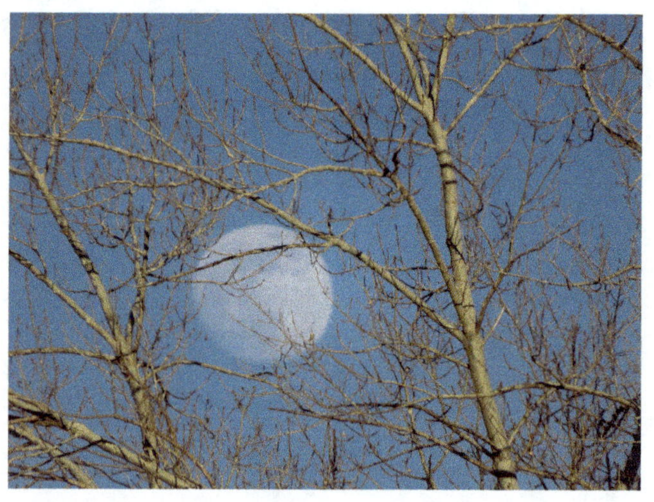

51

Charity

Gift of charity
Given for true purposes
Shadow across time

52

Charity

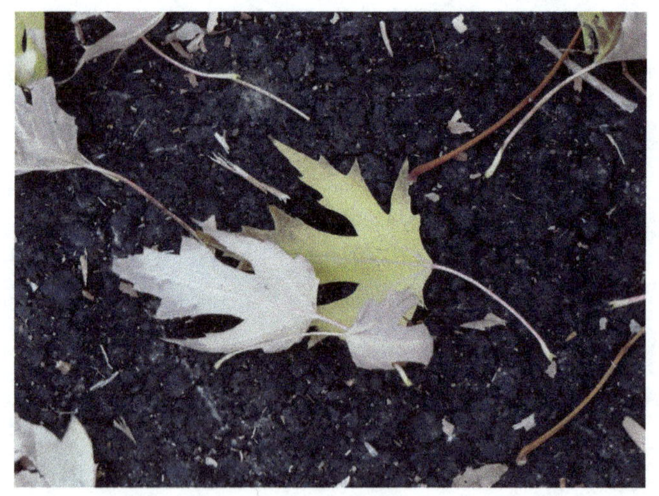

***

53

Faith

When life is darkest
Worry; what will happen next
Faith; see water flow

54

Faith

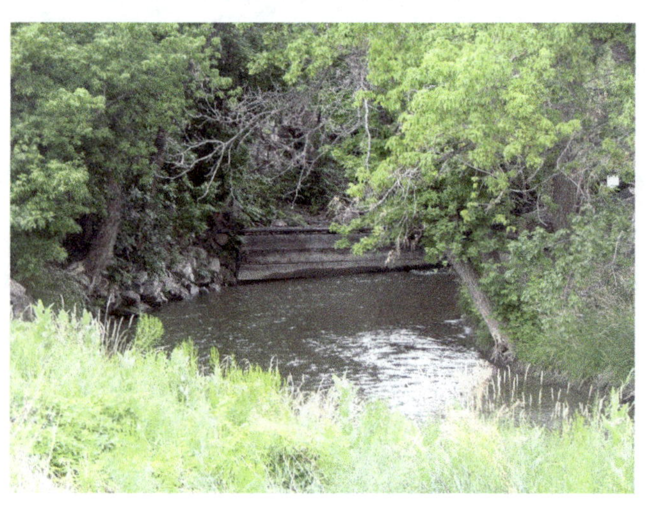

55

Journey

Wonderful journey
Despite heartache, pain, and loss
Watching for blessings

56

Journey

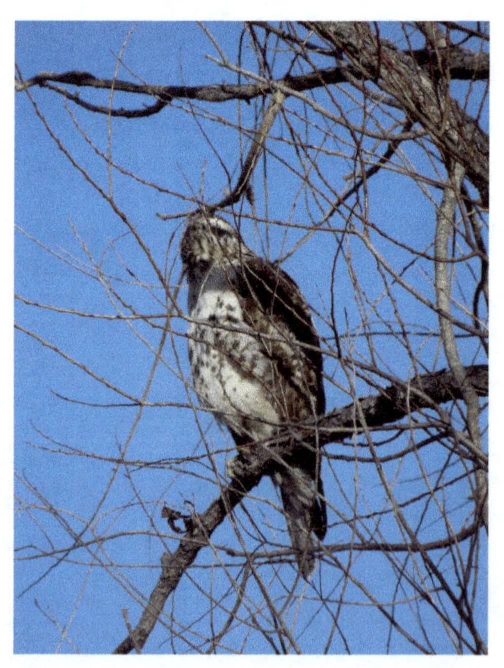

57

Fall In Bloom

Fall colors in bloom
Lessons from nature's grand plan
Grow until you're done

58

Fall In Bloom

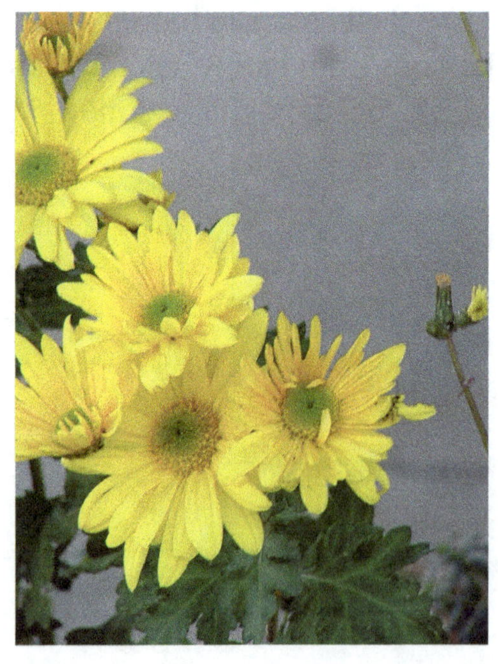

59

Summer's End

Phoenix in ashes
All we knew is gone from sight
Fall cycle rises

60

Summer's End

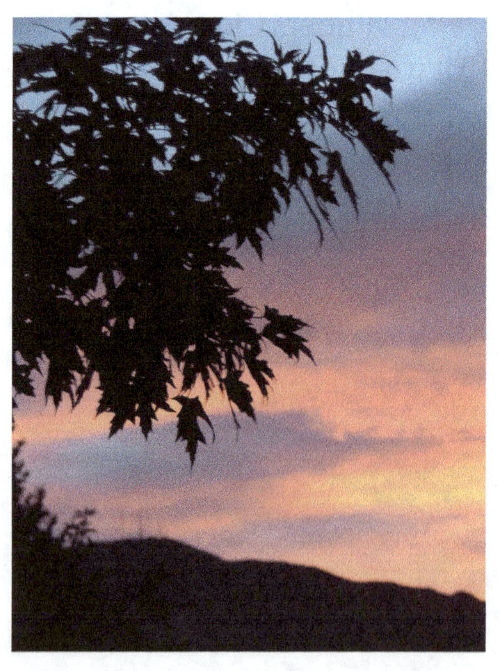

61

Life

Explaining a life
Waters change but do not change
Is it good or bad

62

Life

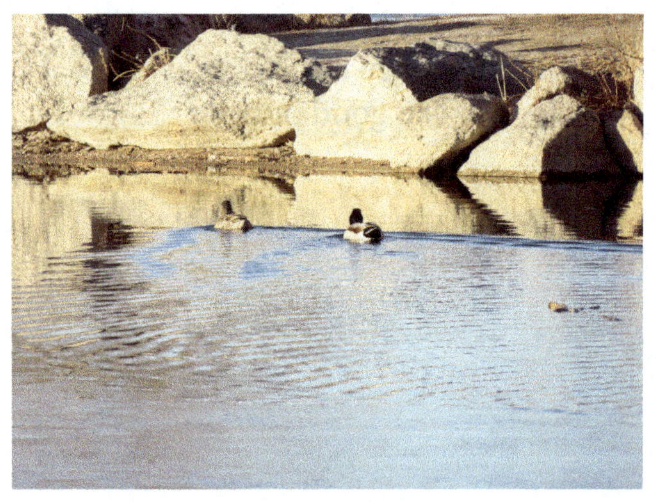

63

Eventide

Soft cool wood-tinged air
Eventide cast its magic
Comfort is at hand

64

Eventide

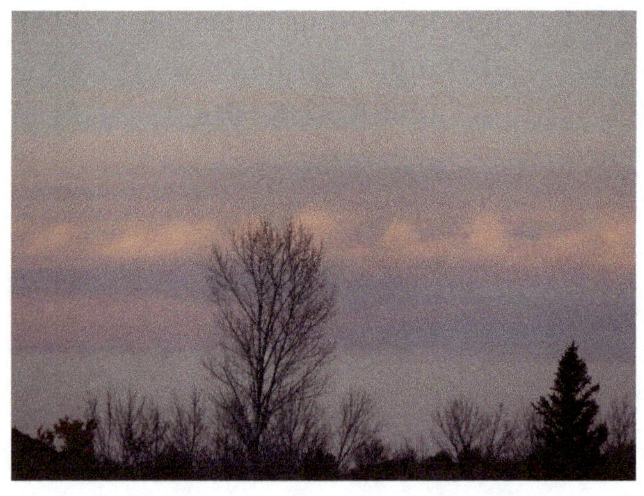

65

Now

Now is forever
Life cannot be repeated
Even mountains change

66

Now

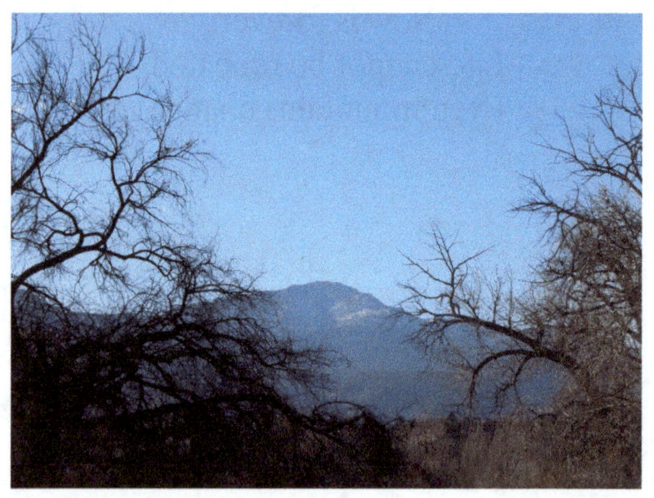

67

Courage

Courage not fear
Otherwise, you miss living
Savor day's blessing

68

Courage

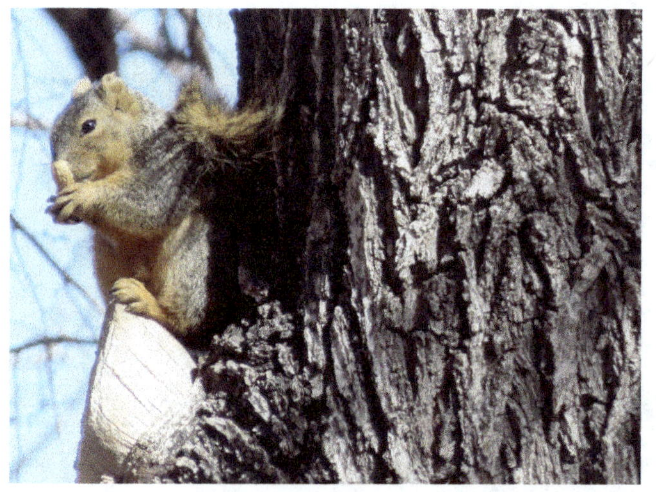

69

Chinook

Icy winter wind
Cutting through all like a knife
Chinook wind behind

70

Chinook

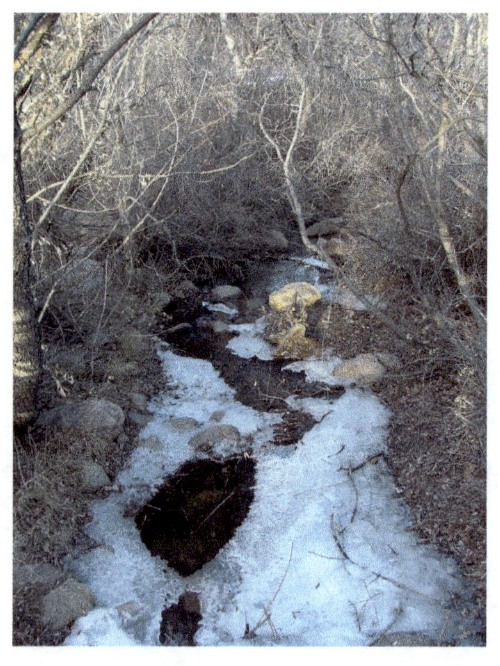

71

Special Memories

Walk upon the earth
Create special memories
Step by precious step

72

Special Memories

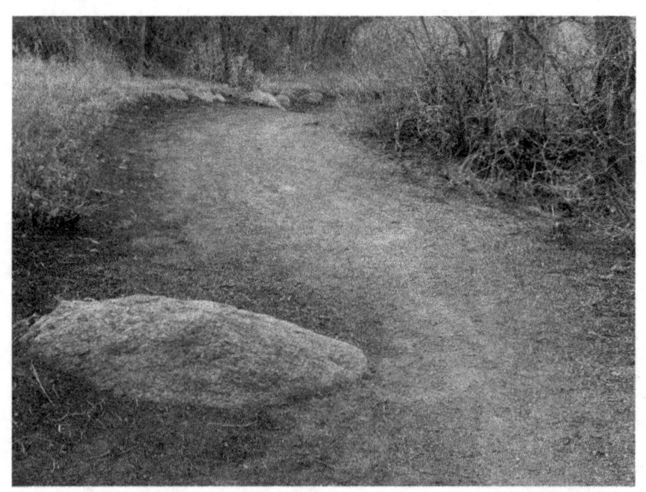

73

Seasons

Earlier sunsets
Another season closing
Joy, fresh adventures

74

Seasons

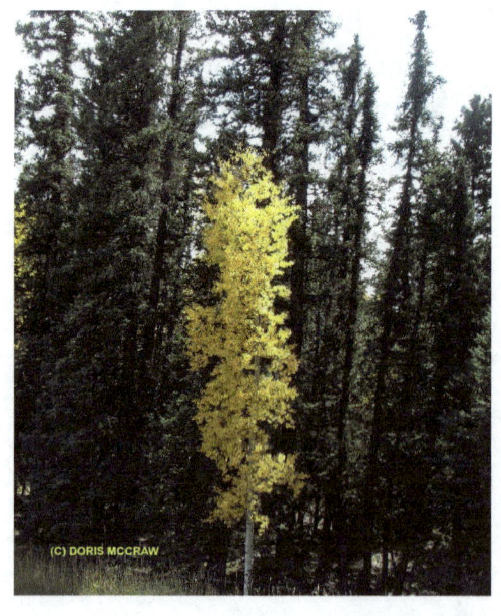

75

Ending

Where will it all end
High, low, or straight line action
Just mountains to cross

76

Ending

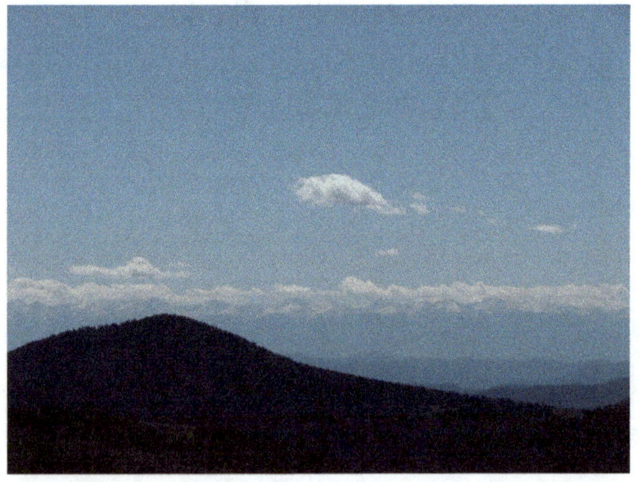

77

Appause

A stage is empty
Just remembering applause
Life's a waning moon

78

Appause

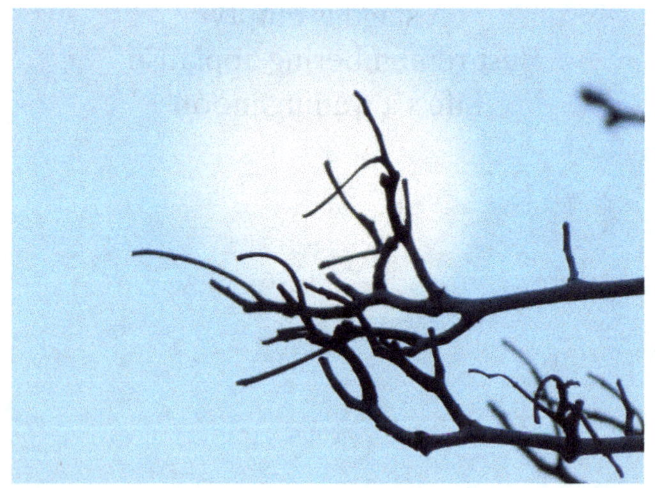

79

True Strength

Defining true strength
Guarding aspen, stately pine
Symbiotic life

80

True Strength

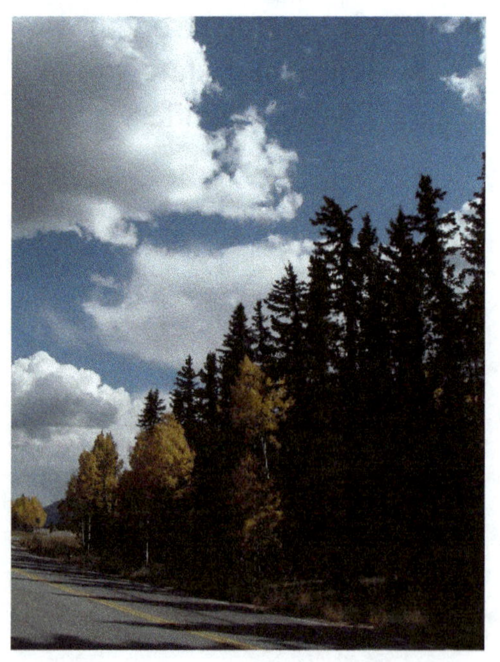

81

Life's Adventure

Life's rich adventure
Unimagined clear sailing
On white fluffy clouds

82

Life's Adventure

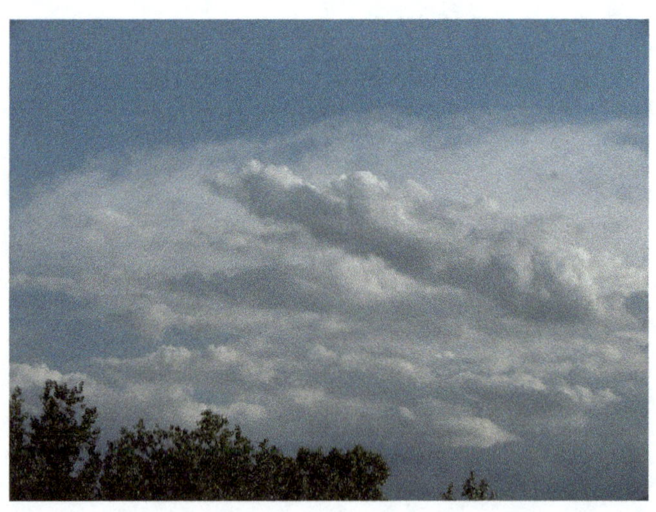

83

Older

As we grow older
Priorities seem to change
Taking leaps of faith

84

Older

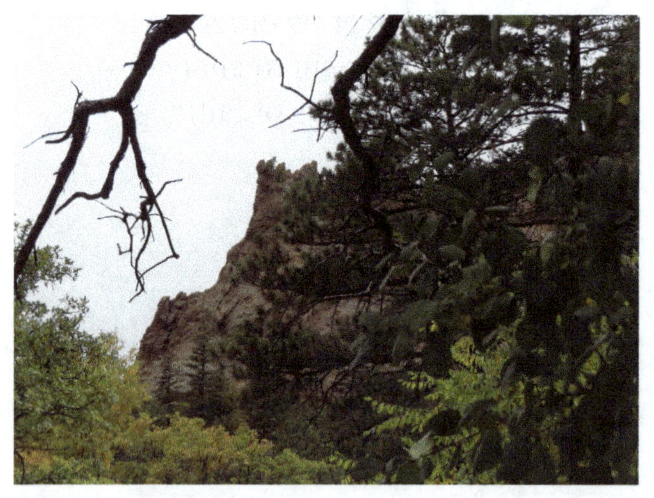

85

Hiding

All hiding something
Perfection will never be
Just see the beauty

86

Hiding

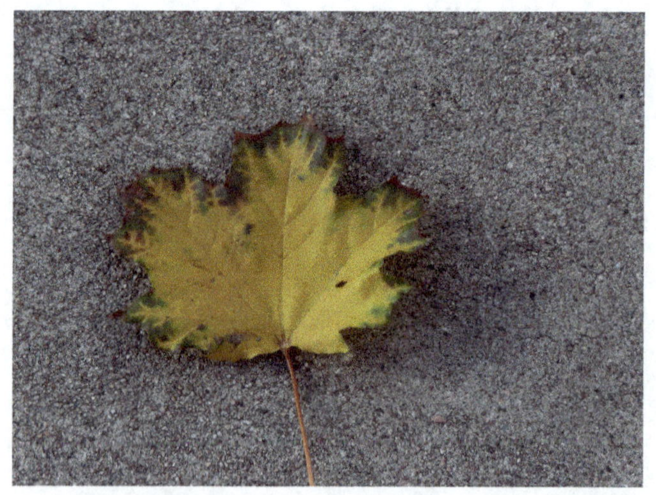

87

Balance

Balancing the scale
People more than bottom line
Beauty free to all

88

Balance

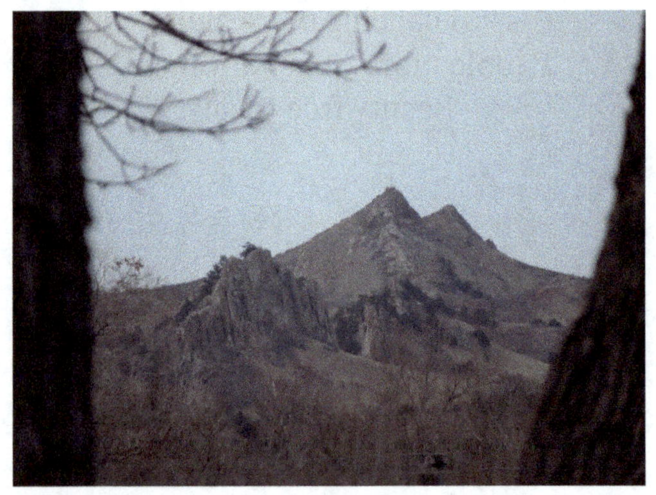

89

Precious Petal

Each precious petal
Unique individual
Together, stunning

90

Precious Petal

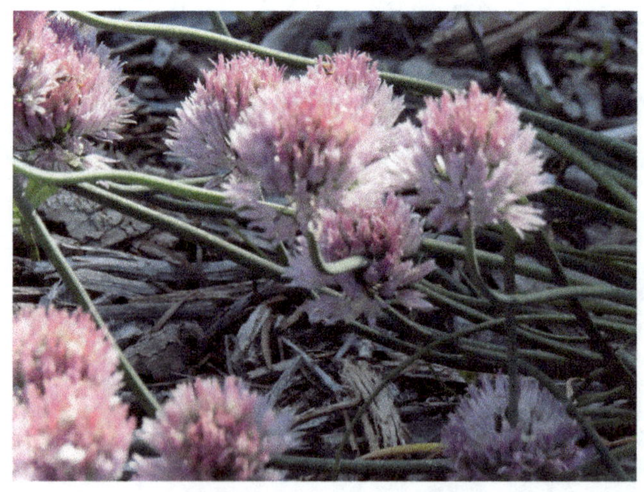

91

Overabundant

Overabundant
Extreme expression abound
Arid land's beauty

92

Overabundant

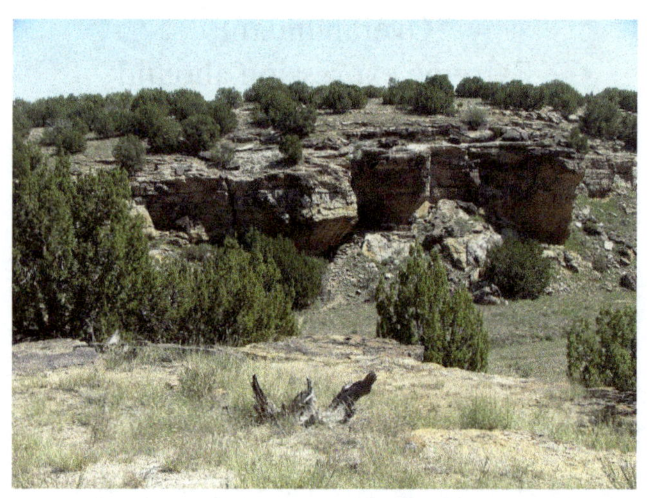

93

Gift Of Gold

Gift of gold sunshine
Gentle refreshing breezes
Special everyday

94

Gift Of Gold

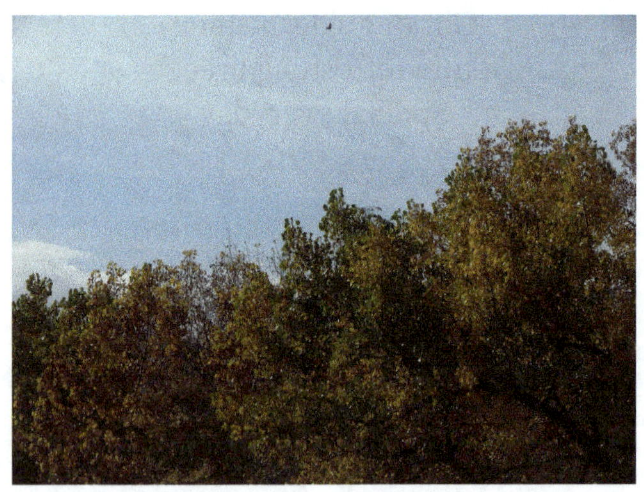

95

Random Thoughts

Wayward random thoughts
Like scores of bright-hued flowers
Wild, yet beautiful

96

Random Thoughts

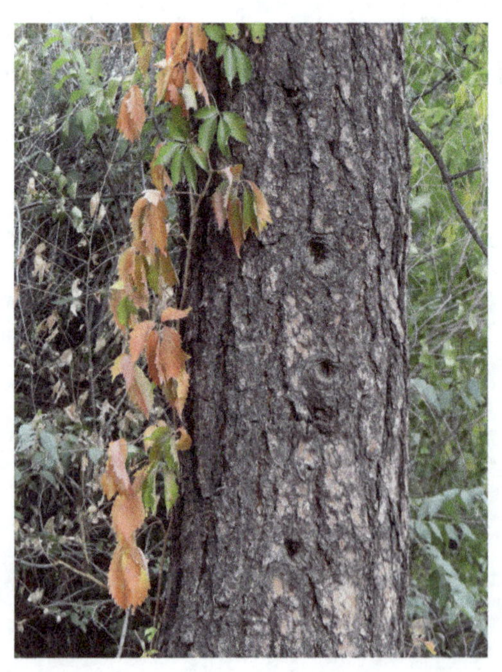

97

Lighter Note

On a lighter note
Birds singing, a gentle breeze
Contented with life

98

Lighter Note

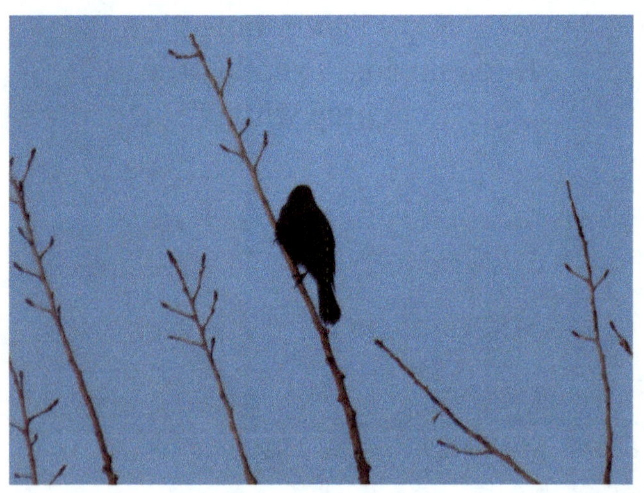

99

Prejudged

To prejudge something
Basing fact on a fiction
The world through filters

100

Prejudged

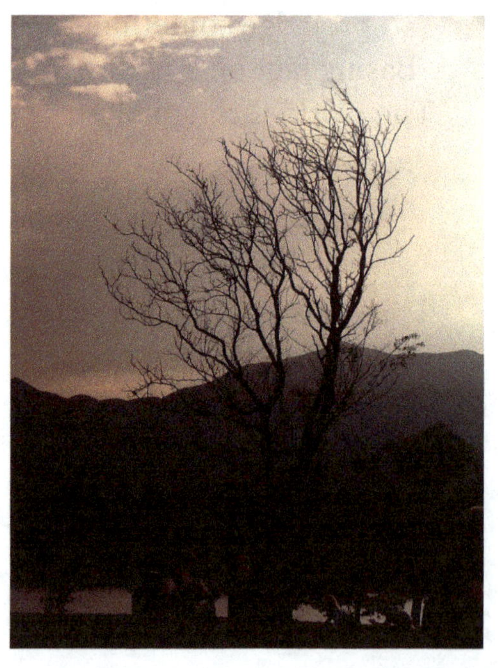

101

Now

Now is forever.
It cannot be repeated.
Even mountains change

102

Now

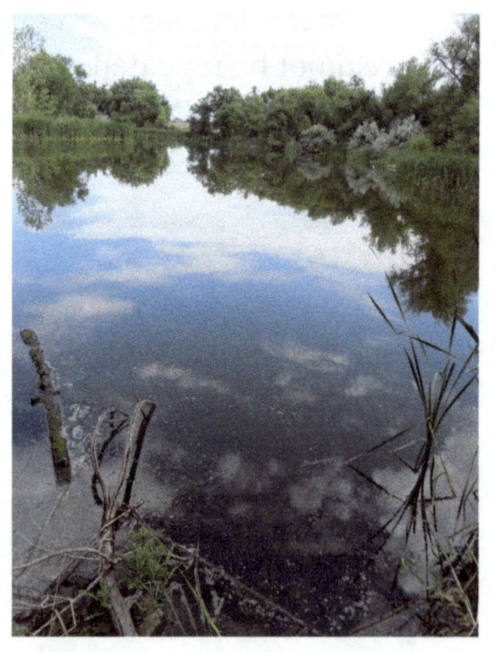

103

Surprise

Softly evening comes
A surprise for the busy
Counting time well spent

104

Surprise

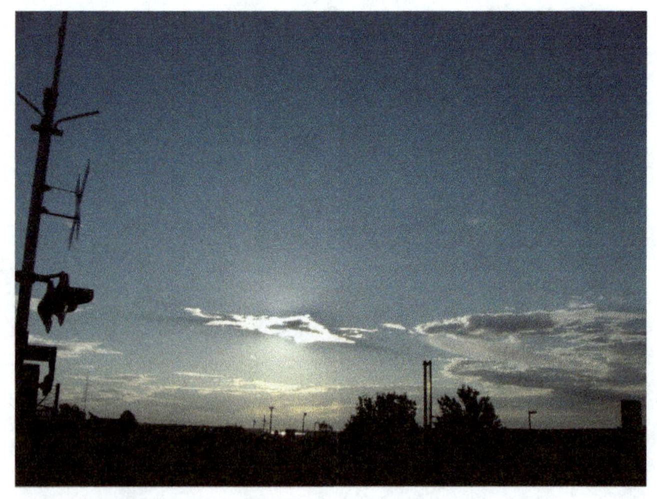

Afterword

Thank you for reading 52 Haiku. If you enjoyed the poems and photos, please share your thoughts either in a review or with me at ChinookMountainPublishi ng@gmail.com

Haiku was a writing practice I fell in love with. I was already in love with photography and the chance to combine these two loves was too good a chance to pass up. The words are also an homage to the author Helen (Hunt) Jackson. I became enamored with Jackson's work as I took on the challenge of presenting her works and story to the world as an actor/recreator. While a different form of poetry, the emotions, and stories that are told by a poet can strike deep into one's psyche as Helen's did mine.

About the Author

Doris A. McCraw is a mid-westerner who found her home at the foot of Pikes Peak in the Rocky Mountains of Colorado. As a child, she would sit and listen to the stories of those around her. It was the beginning of a lifelong passion to find and share the stories of those who preceded her.

The midwest where she grew up was filled with stories of pioneers who braved the wilderness to build forts, towns, and businesses. The Mississippi River, near her hometown, also inspired a love of nature.

Her poetry and fiction writing also came from history. As Helen (Hunt) Jackson she learned a new appreciation for the world around her. It also inspired Doris to pursue publication to continue to share her passion for the world around her.

Doris loves the haiku form of poetry, the structure, and rhythm. It also lends itself to the photography Doris enjoys while taking in the sights, trails, and uniqueness that is Colorado.

Also By

"Under the Stone: Early Women Doctors in Evergreen Cemetery"

As fiction author Angela Raines:

Kiowa Wells Stories:

Book One – *"Josie's Dream"*

Book Two – *"Chasing A Chance"*

Book Three- *"The Outlaw's Letter"*

Additional work:

"Home for His Heart" - an Agate Gulch novella

"Never Had A Chance" – An Agate Gulch novella

"Gift of Forgiveness" – An Agate Gulch novella

"Lost Knight" - A Medieval Novella

Works in Anthologies:

"Under Western Stars" – Western Anthology

"The Untamed West" – Western Anthology

"One Hot Knight" – Medieval Anthology

"One Yuletide Knight" – Medieval Anthology

"One Christmas Knight" – Medieval Anthology

Also By

www.ingramcontent.com/pod-product-compliance
Lightning Source LLC
LaVergne TN
LVHW010355160826
845677LV00005BA/1287

* 9 7 9 8 3 5 6 2 7 3 6 5 0 *